# BRITAIN
## IN OLD PHOTOGRAPHS

# AROUND
# SHEFFIELD

## Then & Now

### GEOFFREY HOWSE

SUTTON PUBLISHING

Sutton Publishing Limited
Phoenix Mill · Thrupp · Stroud
Gloucestershire · GL5 2BU

First published 2002

*Title page photograph*: This 1830s engraved view of Sheffield from the south-east shows just how open the city was before industrial expansion in the steel industry saw the creation of suburbs, which covered the surrounding hillsides and valleys with housing estates, factories and shops. *(Courtesy of John Bishop)*

**British Library Cataloguing in Publication Data**
A catalogue record for this book is available from the British Library.

ISBN 0-7509-2994-4

Typeset in 10.5/13.5 Photina.
Typesetting and origination by
Sutton Publishing Limited.
Printed and bound in England by
J.H. Haynes & Co. Ltd, Sparkford.

Rivelin Valley, *c.* 1910. This is a famous beauty spot, situated to the west of the city. *(Bryan Woodriff Collection)*

# CONTENTS

The Adelphi, Attercliffe. This building has enjoyed a varied existence since it opened in 1908. Occasionally live performances took place but cinema was its mainstay from its opening. By the 1960s bingo was the main attraction. Since 1998 the Adelphi has operated as a night club and live entertainment venue. It also serves as a training area for the music industry. *(Paul T. Langley Welch)*

A present day view of Meadow Hall, from the railway embankment. The prestigious Meadowhall Shopping Centre has, since its opening in September 1990, remained the most successful shopping complex in Europe, although not the largest. This enormous American-style shopping mall was built on the site of Hadfield's East Hecla Works, one of Sheffield's famous steel manufacturing plants. The Meadowhall complex also contains a cinema village and attracts visitors from many parts of the country. *(Paul T. Langley Welch)*

# INTRODUCTION

There have been many books written about Sheffield and district. Some are scholarly, some are great tomes packed with information that is difficult to sift through; others take the form of pamphlets, or guide books, and then there are those which are usually categorised as coffee table books, often comprising just a few facts strung together with illustrations. Then there are those self-published or vanity-published books, made so much easier to produce with the advent of the photocopier and the computer. Indeed, so great is the diversity of material available that the casual reader is spoilt for choice. This book is a combination of several elements. The material contained within its pages has been a matter of personal choice. The title could be seen as misleading. Indeed, my accusers may have a valid point. However, in my defence I would argue that such is the diversity of the area 'around Sheffield' that if I were to produce fifty such volumes it is unlikely that I would be able to scratch beyond the surface of the vast wealth of historical fact which the area contains. We all have our particular favourite subjects and sometimes

An early twentieth-century view of the New Road, Rivelin Valley. (*Bryan Woodriff Collection*)

when a book is published there is great disappointment when a particular element has been left out. As this book is dependent on the availability of pictures, I would go on to say that the publishing of many similar volumes would only contain the history of any area up to the point that the work was completed, and that within days of submitting the work to the printing press, dramatic events or the unearthing of some new facts or indeed artefacts could render the work out of date before it was even published. I have based my choice on those images which are most appealing from a visual point of view or which have some historic importance. I have also chosen to show, in some instances, different aspects of the same subject, particularly where postcard images are concerned. This is because it is important to be able to compare changes, angles, views or aspects, even within a short time frame.

As for my qualifications for writing about this area: I was born in Sheffield. However, I cannot claim to be a Sheffielder. My birth took place in the late afternoon of 24 October 1955, at Jessops Hospital for Women, sometime between 4.30p.m. and 5.30p.m.; I know this as my mother complains that she missed her afternoon tea as a result of me making an appearance. Shortly after my birth I was taken to the family home in Elsecar and my connection with Sheffield came to an end, as far as being a resident was concerned.

This is my fifth book about the Sheffield area. I do not claim to be a great historian, nor indeed would I consider myself an authority on local affairs. My efforts so far have been largely concentrated on the city of Sheffield itself, with the odd sortie into the suburbs or satellite towns and villages. This book is my first attempt to show some of the different aspects of the area surrounding Sheffield. Although I have not adhered strictly to north, south, east and west, I have by and large tried to include areas within those compass

The Botanical Gardens, Sheffield, *c.* 1905. (*Bryan Woodriff Collection*)

Warren Lane Methodist chapel, Chapeltown, Harvest Festival, 1952. Among those featured in the photograph are Mr Hill (Superintendent), wearing glasses, Mrs Jackson, Mrs Bassinder, Grace Lambert, Jean Goddard, Rosemary Harrison, Catherine Hindley, Carol Hopson, Miss Chapman, Patricia Waite and Miss Denton. *(Courtesy of Mrs Joan Hopson)*

points. I would have liked to include other places but sometimes the non-availability of suitable material makes it impossible. If you have any photographs that help to fill gaps please contact me via the publisher.

The area within the ancient manor of Hallam, and the region known as Hallamshire which includes Sheffield and district, contains a considerable amount of history. Sheffield itself was granted a city charter in 1893. As a settlement it had existed long before the Romans came to Britain. They built a road into Derbyshire and a fort at Wincobank. In 829 the Anglian kings of Northumberland and Mercia met at Dore to settle their differences. The Normans built a castle on the site now occupied by Castle Market. This was replaced by another and eventually came into the ownership of the earls of Shrewsbury. The castle, along with many other such Royalist strongholds, was destroyed in the aftermath of the Civil War. But what of the towns and villages that surround what has become the fourth largest city in England? They have all played their part in one way or another, some more significantly than others. I hope I have managed to capture some of the essence of this remarkable area and I sincerely hope that the reader enjoys my efforts.

*Geoffrey Howse, July 2002*

Peace celebration in Manchester Road, Stocksbridge, November 1918. *(Sheffield Central Library)*

Manchester Road, Stocksbridge, April 2002. *(Paul T. Langley Welch)*

# 1
# Around the City

The Orchard Square clock, which celebrates
Sheffield's long association with the cutlery and
steel industries. *(Paul T. Langley Welch)*

Sir Marcus Samuel Bt (later Lord Bearsted), Lord Mayor of London, laid the foundation stone of the University of Sheffield buildings in 1903. Constructed to the designs of architect E. Mitchel Gibbs, Sheffield University was opened by Their Majesties King Edward Vll and Queen Alexandra on 12 July 1905. The university buildings are seen here from Weston Park. The octagonal Edgar Allen Library seen on the right, also designed by E. Mitchel Gibbs, was added in 1909–11. The statue is of Ebenezer Elliott (1787–1849), the 'Corn Law Rhymer', also known as the 'Poor Man's Poet'. *(Bryan Woodriff Collection)*

Sheffield University, from a similar spot to the photograph above. The war memorial is to the officers, NCOs and men of the York and Lancaster Regiment. An inscription shows that 8,814 men lost their lives (1914–19), as did 1,222 men from the regiment who fell (1939–45). The author can be glimpsed admiring the monument from the bushes in the left foreground. *(Paul T. Langley Welch)*

Sheffield University, *c.* 1914. *(Bryan Woodriff Collection)*

Sheffield University
buildings, April 2002.
*(Paul T. Langley Welch)*

Sheffield University, 1970s. *(Bryan Woodriff Collection)*

The Mappin Art Gallery, Weston Park. Built at a cost of £15,000 between 1886 and 1888, to the designs of architects Flockton and Gibbs, it has a long colonnaded front in the Ionic order and was founded under the terms of the will of John Newton Mappin, a wealthy cutlery manufacturer, who bequeathed 153 paintings. His nephew, Sir Frederick Mappin, presented a further 48 paintings. Further bequests followed. Today the Mappin Gallery has an impressive collection of paintings and holds regular exhibitions. Adjacent to the Mappin Gallery is the City Museum, which holds the finest collection of cutlery in the world. The Mappin Gallery and Weston Park is seen here in the early twentieth century. *(Bryan Woodriff Collection)*

*Opposite*: The Edgar Allen Library and University buildings in April 2002. The South Gate of Weston Park can be seen to the left of the library. *(Paul T. Langley Welch)*

An early twentieth-century view of the principal façade of the Mappin Gallery. *(Bryan Woodriff Collection)*

The Mappin Gallery viewed from Weston Park, April 2002. *(Paul T. Langley Welch)*

A 1960s view of the Mappin Gallery. Note the recently planted conifer in the right foreground. *(Bryan Woodriff Collection)*

The Mappin Gallery in April 2002, from the same spot as seen above. The little conifer in that image has grown into a giant in the thirty-odd years that has intervened. *(Paul T. Langley Welch)*

The Mount, seen here during renovation in May 1959, was built between 1830 and 1832 to the designs of Sheffield architect William Flockton to emulate a country house. Seventeen bays long and two and a half storeys high with a central pediment of six giant Ionic columns, and pavilions with a pair of Ionic pilasters to each, this graceful building was in fact eight substantial houses. It was nicknamed Flockton's Folly because its situation overlooking Glossop Road at Broomhill was considered to be too far out of town to be of interest to buyers – who would have needed substantial means to purchase such a home. The Mount proved to be no folly but became a popular place to live. One of its first residents was the noted poet and hymn writer James Montgomery, who moved to the Mount in 1835 and died there in 1854. *(Sheffield Central Library)*

The Mount, in April 2002.
In the early 1940s the entire
building was purchased by
John Walsh Limited, when
their department store in High
Street was bombed in the
Sheffield blitz. In 1958 it was
acquired by United Steels and
it eventually became the
regional headquarters of the
British Steel Corporation. They
sold it in 1978, and it is now
divided into offices. The
curious structure which stands
in front of The Mount dates
from the time when the British
Steel Corporation occupied the
premises. It almost completely
ruins the view of this fine
building and makes The Mount
itself difficult to photograph.
*(Paul T. Langley Welch)*

A view of the Sir Frederick Mappin Building, part of the University of Sheffield, from St George's Square, 1924.
*(David J. Richardson Collection)*

*Below*: A contemporary view of the Sir Frederick Mappin Building. The saplings of 1924 have grown considerably and when in full leaf almost completely obscure the elegant proportions of Mappin's building. *(Paul T. Langley Welch)*

The curiously shaped extension to Sheffield's Gothic Town Hall, built between 1973 and 1977, seen from the Peace Gardens. *(Paul T. Langley Welch)*

At the beginning of 2002 the demolition of Sheffield's much-criticised Town Hall extension began. This mid-April 2002 view shows the same site as the previous photograph, from the same spot in the Peace Gardens. The new Winter Gardens complex is being constructed. Once completed, the building will house one of the most impressive collections of plants from temperate regions to be seen in Northern England. It will be possible for the public to walk under cover through walkways which link Arundel Gate, the Millennium Galleries, the Winter Gardens and the Peace Gardens. *(Paul T. Langley Welch)*

St Paul's church, Pinstone Street, at the beginning of the twentieth century. This church was built to serve as a chapel-of-ease to the nearby medieval parish church of St Peter (now the Cathedral Church of St Peter and St Paul). The church was built by public subscription, and the first stone was laid on 28 May 1720. St Paul's was built to the designs of Ralph Tunnicliffe of Dalton, assisted by John Platt (the elder), in the Baroque style and completed in 1721. It remained closed for worship for nineteen years, owing to a dispute about who should appoint the curate. The dome on top of the tower was added in 1769. After the raising of the parish church to cathedral status in 1914, and owing to the shift in population from the city centre to the suburbs, many city churches became redundant. In 1936 it was decided that some churches had to be demolished. Despite being considered the finest Georgian building in the city, St Paul's was demolished that same year. The Peace Gardens were created after the Second World War on the site of the church and churchyard, although the removal of human remains did not take place until the new Peace Gardens were laid out in 1998. *(Sheffield Central Library)*

The Peace Gardens today, showing the site of St Paul's church. *(Paul T. Langley Welch)*

# 2

# The Southern Outskirts

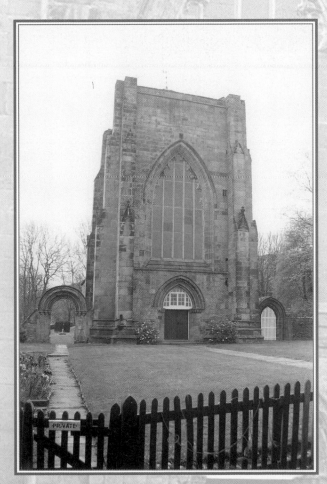

Beauchief Abbey, April 2002. *(Paul T. Langley Welch)*

Early lords in the late Middle Ages in Hallamshire were the Furnivals. A reminder of that family is the area known as Furnival Gate in the city centre. The male line of the Furnival family came to an end towards the close of the fourteenth century. Early in the fifteenth century the Talbots became established in Sheffield, after John Talbot, the owner of considerable lands in Shropshire, had married Maud Nevill, daughter and heiress of Sir Thomas Nevill and Joan de Furnival. The Talbot family dominated the area for over two hundred years from their castle in Sheffield and their Manor Lodge. Only fragments of Sheffield Castle remain beneath today's Castle Market in the city centre, but there are more substantial remains of Manor Lodge. Originally a hunting lodge in the old deer park, and in use since at least the beginning of the last quarter of the fifteenth century, it was converted into a large country house. The first of the Talbots, John, served in Ireland as Lord Lieutenant from 1414 to 1419 and took charge of the English army in France in 1428. His military achievements earned him high honours: firstly he was created a Knight of the Garter, and in 1442 he was raised to the peerage as the Earl of Shrewsbury.

The lst Earl of Shrewsbury died in battle in France in 1453. His son, the 2nd Earl, also called John, died in the Battle of Northampton in 1460. The first three earls of

The Turret House, the only part of the once extensive Manor Lodge to survive intact, *c.* 1900. *(Bryan Woodriff Collection)*

The Turret House, Manor Lodge, April 2002. *(Paul T. Langley Welch)*

Shrewsbury did not spend much of their time on what they regarded as one of their lesser estates. It was George Talbot, 4th Earl of Shrewsbury (1468–1538) who decided to make his principal home in Sheffield. He did not consider the two-hundred-year-old Sheffield Castle fashionable enough and decided to improve the hunting lodge within his deer park, upgrading it to a substantial country house. In 1530 Cardinal Wolsey spent eighteen days there. He died four days after his visit, at Leicester. On the 4th Earl's death his body was buried in Sheffield parish church, in the chapel he had built (still known as the Shrewsbury chapel) in today's cathedral church of St Peter and St Paul. Francis, the 5th Earl, was born at Sheffield Castle in 1500. He occupied various important positions including President of the Council of the North, and was a member of the Privy Council at the Court of Queen Elizabeth I. He continued to build at Sheffield Lodge and exerted a great deal of influence locally. George Talbot, the 6th Earl (c. 1528–90), became even more powerful than his predecessors: he was a member of the Privy Council, Lieutenant-General for Yorkshire, Nottinghamshire and Derbyshire, and, following the execution of the Duke of Norfolk in 1572, Earl Marshal of England. He married twice, his second wife being that celebrated Elizabethan Bess of Hardwick. On his marriage to Bess he acquired a life interest in Chatsworth House but despite having large estates in eleven counties and London, which included three castles, Sheffield Manor Lodge remained his favourite seat, and he and his wife Bess spent a great deal of money enlarging it and improving the gardens.

A late nineteenth-century view of the ruins of Manor Lodge. (*Bryan Woodriff Collection*)

A view of the ruins of Manor Lodge taken just a few years after the previous image. It shows the extent of the decay which took place, and the measures taken to prevent any further damage. The roof timbers are gone and a considerable amount of masonry has also disappeared. Some attempt to preserve what remains of the structure has clearly been made by capping loose stonework. *(Bryan Woodriff Collection)*

After the arrest of Mary Queen of Scots in 1569, Elizabeth I appointed her loyal subject George, 6th Earl of Shrewsbury, as her custodian. The Queen of Scots was brought to Sheffield and remained in his charge from 1570 to 1584. She was mainly imprisoned at Sheffield Castle and Sheffield Manor Lodge but from time to time was moved to Buxton or Chatsworth and once to Worksop. Although many accounts mention the Turret House being her place of incarceration while at Manor Lodge, and that it had been especially built for that purpose, this was in fact not the case. During this long period of incarceration the marriage of the Earl and Bess of Hardwick broke down. Bess eventually moved to her birthplace at Hardwick Hall and began building a new hall adjacent to her old family home. George moved to Handsworth where he lived openly with his mistress. He died at Sheffield Manor Lodge in 1590. Bess outlived him by seventeen years. George's son, Gilbert (1553–1616), succeeded him as the 7th Earl. He became a prominent figure at court.

After Gilbert died, having had no sons, and his only brother dying soon afterwards, the title passed to a distant relative. Gilbert's estates were shared between his three daughters. His youngest daughter inherited the Yorkshire and Derbyshire properties. She married Thomas Howard, Earl of Arundel and Surrey. Her grandson was created the 5th Duke of Norfolk (the Howards having forfeited that title in 1572).

A similar view of the ruins of Manor Lodge to that on page 31, April 2002. Shortly after the Howards inherited their estates in Yorkshire Sheffield Castle was completely destroyed on the instructions of Parliament in 1649–50, when they ordered that all castles that had been fortified by the Royalists during the Civil War should be demolished. The Manor Lodge was allowed to fall into disrepair. Most of what remained of this once spectacular mansion was dismantled in the early eighteenth century. *(Paul T. Langley Welch)*

The ruins of Manor Lodge, April 2002. *(Paul T. Langley Welch)*

The village of Dore in the early twentieth century: one of the loveliest villages in the Sheffield area and a very desirable spot in which to live. *(Courtesy of Chris Sharp of Old Barnsley)*

A view of the same spot, April 2001. *(Paul T. Langley Welch)*

Midland Railway construction at Dore and Totley railway station, *c.* 1900. *(Sheffield Central Library)*

A similar view, May 1968. *(Sheffield Central Library)*

Dore station as it is now called, April 2002. *(Paul T. Langley Welch)*

Hillfoot Road, Totley, *c.* 1900. The house in the right foreground was known as Avalon. The Victorian villas on the hillside on the left are called Doris and Vera. *(Courtesy of Chris Sharp of Old Barnsley)*

Mature trees, dense undergrowth and barbed wire prevent us being able to take an exact comparison to the previous image. The old house Avalon has been replaced by another which bears the same name, albeit in a slightly different position to the original. Doris and Vera are still there, obscured by the trees. *(Paul T. Langley Welch)*

Ye Old Cross Scythes Hotel, Totley, *c.* 1900. *(Courtesy of Chris Sharp of Old Barnsley)*

A century later, April 2002, this historic hotel is called simply Cross Scythes. What a pity! *(Paul T. Langley Welch)*

Ye Old Cross Scythes Hotel, during the First World War. Notice the changes to the entrance made since the turn of the century. *(Courtesy of Chris Sharp of Old Barnsley)*

The Cross Scythes from the same spot, April 2002. *(Paul T. Langley Welch)*

Abbeydale Industrial Hamlet, seen here in the 1980s and situated 4 miles from the city centre, close to the River Sheaf, between Beauchief and Dore. It dates from the eighteenth century and contains workshops, warehouses and cottages. Now an industrial museum, Abbeydale Industrial Hamlet has a rich history and for most of the nineteenth century was a major agricultural tool-producing complex. With its four waterwheels, water-driven tilt forge and grinding wheel and unique crucible steel furnace, it is the first industrial site to be given Grade I listing by English Heritage. *(Sheffield Central Library)*

Workshops at Abbeydale Industrial Hamlet. *(Sheffield City Library)*

A 1980s view of Abbeydale Industrial Hamlet. *(Bryan Woodriff Collection)*

Abbeydale Industrial Hamlet, April 2002. *(Paul T. Langley Welch)*

The Kirk family installing their Anderson shelter at 33 Firbeck Road, Woodseats, 4 September 1940. The first air raid warning actually came during the night of 4/5 September, encouraging the family to complete the work on the shelter. Mrs Kirk stands in the foreground, while Mr Kirk is assisted by his twelve-year-old daughter June Mary Kirk (now Mrs Firth). *(Courtesy of Mrs J.M. Firth and Sheffield Central Library)*

The garden of 33 Firbeck Road, April 2002. Now reduced in size, the part where the Kirk family's Anderson shelter stood is behind the fence. *(Paul T. Langley Welch)*

No. 33 Firbeck Road, Woodseats. Today it is the home of the Jepson family. *(Paul T. Langley Welch)*

The Big Tree Hotel, Chesterfield Road, Woodseats, *c.* 1900. The eighteenth-century inn seen here was formerly called the Masons Arms. A large horse chestnut tree stands in the forecourt, from which the public house took its name. *(Sheffield Central Library)*

The Big Tree, Woodseats, March 1991. There is still a big tree in the forecourt but it is a sorry specimen compared with the tree in 1900. *(Sheffield Central Library)*

The Big Tree, Woodseats, April 2002. In 1996 the horse chestnut tree finally succumbed to the ravages of time and was replaced by a new tree, little more than a sapling. Six years later that tree has grown considerably. Perhaps at the turn of the next century it might justifiably be called The Big Tree once again. *(Paul T. Langley Welch)*

# 3

# The Western Outskirts

Rivelin Valley, Sheffield, *c.* 1900. *(Author's Collection)*

Sheffield Barracks, Hillsborough, *c.* 1900. *(Bryan Woodriff Collection)*

Sheffield Barracks, Hillsborough, April 2002. This distinctive landmark no longer serves a military purpose. In recent years the old complex of barrack buildings has been converted into a supermarket, public house, speciality shops and offices. *(Paul T. Langley Welch)*

Sheffield Barracks, Hillsborough, April 2002. *(Paul T. Langley Welch)*

Withens Avenue, Hillsborough, *c.* 1910. *(Courtesy of Chris Sharp of Old Barnsley)*

Withens Avenue, Hillsborough, April 2002. *(Paul T. Langley Welch)*

An early twentieth-century view of Rockley Road, Hillsborough. *(Courtesy of Chris Sharp of Old Barnsley)*

Rockley Road, Hillsborough, April 2002. Much of the former elegance of these well-proportioned semi-detached villas has been marred by the ubiquitous plastic windows. The right-hand side of the street has been developed in a mish-mash of styles, from the 1920s onwards. *(Paul T. Langley Welch)*

Wadsley lies on the north-western edge of Sheffield on one of the seven hills on which the city was built. Some of the substantial late Victorian villas in Wadsley Lane are seen here in the early Edwardian period. *(Courtesy of Chris Sharp of Old Barnsley)*

Wadsley Lane from the same spot as in the picture above, April 2002. *(Paul T. Langley Welch)*

Wharncliffe Side is a small village 6 miles to the north-north-west of Sheffield, where once file cutters plied their trade. Situated in the valley nestling beneath Wharncliffe Craggs and forming part of the Wharncliffe Estate, Wharncliffe Side is a community of just over 2,500 people. This view of Wharncliffe Side dates from *c.* 1920. *(Courtesy of Chris Sharp of Old Barnsley)*

Wharncliffe Side, April 2002. *(Paul T. Langley Welch)*

An early twentieth-century view of Wharncliffe Craggs, once a popular place to visit from Sheffield and the surrounding villages, as well as Barnsley and Rotherham, before road and rail transport made more distant attractions easier to reach. *(Courtesy of Chris Sharp of Old Barnsley)*

The Lodge, Wharnciffe Crags, *c.* 1905. Wharncliffe Lodge was built in the early sixteenth century on top of a crag in the savage wilderness of Wharncliffe Chase. An inscription carved on a nearby rock and recorded in *Some Account of English Deer Parks* by E.P. Shirley, published in 1807, asked the reader to pray for the soul of Sir Thomas Wortley 'which caused a lodge to be made on this crag in the midst of Wharncliffe for his pleasure to hear the hart's bell [the stag's rutting cry], in the year of our Lord, 1510.' *(Bryan Woodriff Collection)*

Church Street,
Oughtibridge, early
twentieth century.
*(Courtesy of Chris Sharp of
Old Barnsley)*

Church Street, Oughtibridge, April 2002. Entering the gates of the parish church of The Ascension in the right foreground are the author and his mother Mrs Doreen Howse. *(Paul T. Langley Welch)*

The post office, Langsett Road South, Oughtibridge, in the early twentieth century. The post office building has a date-stone of 1827. *(Courtesy of Chris Sharp of Old Barnsley)*

Langsett Road South,
Oughtibridge, April 2002.
*(Paul T. Langley Welch)*

This Edwardian view shows
Station Lane, Oughtibridge, and
the magnificent countryside which
completely surrounds it. *(Courtesy
of Chris Sharp of Old Barnsley)*

Station Lane, Oughtibridge,
April 2002. The beauty of the
countryside which surrounds this
settlement is undiminished.
*(Paul T. Langley Welch)*

Low Bradfield is seen here from the bridge in the early twentieth century. *(Author's Collection)*

High Bradfield and Low Bradfield, together with Bradfield Dale, comprise Bradfield. Surrounded by bleak moorland and situated on one of the seven hills which form the 'frame' of Sheffield, Bradfield and vicinity has become known as the Sheffield Lake District, because of the four dams built nearby. Lying 7 miles from the city centre, High Bradfield, where St Nicholas's Church is situated, was once known as Kirkton and Low Bradfield as Netherton. Neither village is mentioned in the Domesday Book but the area is referred to as 'Bradefield' in Papal Bulls of 1141. The church of St Nicholas was erected in 1109. During the reign of Henry I (1100–35), the Knights Hospitallers of Jerusalem were granted lands in the area by William de Lovetot, lord of the manor of Hallam. After the Dissolution of the Monasteries, property in the chapelry of Bradfield was given to the Earl of Shrewsbury. There are still the knights' crosses on corbel stones on some of the older cottages.

The view from the bridge in April 2002. *(Paul T. Langley Welch)*

The land in the Bradfield area is extremely hilly, with steeply sloping fields that made farming very hard. In common with many communities throughout the Sheffield area, the farmers did outwork for the cutlery industry, and other metalworking, including nail making, took place. During the night of 11/12 March 1864 a terrible disaster occurred. Known by some as the Bradfield Flood, others as the Sheffield Flood and to many more locals as 't' Flood', it came about after heavy rain burst the Dale Dyke Dam, and millions of gallons of water wreaked a path of devastation through the Loxley Valley, almost into the centre of Sheffield itself; 240 people lost their lives. Bradfield is one of Sheffield and district's hidden gems. Its relative isolation has kept it off the main tourist trails, but the area still gets its fair share of visitors.

The bridge, Low Bradfield, in the Edwardian period. *(Courtesy of Chris Sharp of Old Barnsley)*

The bridge, Low Bradfield, April 2002. *(Paul T. Langley Welch)*

# 4

# *The Northern Outskirts*

The Methodist chapel, Warren Lane, Chapeltown, April 2002.
*(Paul T. Langley Welch)*

Barnsley Road, Fir Vale, *c.* 1905. St Cuthbert's church stands at the junction of Barnsley Road, which carries on up the hill to Sheffield Lane Top, and Owler Lane. *(Courtesy of Bryan Woodriff)*

Barnsley Road, Fir Vale, April 2002. *(Paul T. Langley Welch)*

A late Victorian view of the old Pheasant Inn, Sheffield Lane Top. *(Courtesy of Bryan Woodriff)*

The Pheasant Inn, Sheffield Lane Top, which replaced the old inn seen above, on the same site. Here is how it looked in the early twentieth century. *(Sheffield Central Library)*

The Pheasant Inn, Sheffield Lane Top, April 2002. Hadfield House Lane goes off to the right, Elm Lane to the left and Barnsley Road continues past the front of the Pheasant Inn, then down the hill into Highgreave and on to Ecclesfield. *(Paul T. Langley Welch)*

Situated in Barnsley Road, Sheffield Lane Top, further down the hill from the Pheasant Inn, which is on the opposite side of the road, was the Forum Cinema, seen here in the 1950s. The Forum was built to the designs of architect George Coles and opened in 1938. It eventually changed its name to the Essoldo and closed its doors as a cinema on 31 May 1969. (*Courtesy of Bryan Woodriff*)

The former cinema, seen here in April 2002, is occupied by the United Carpet Mill. The parade of shops which stood next to the cinema has been replaced by a petrol station and car wash. (*Paul T. Langley Welch*)

The fountain and triangular pond, Firth Park, early twentieth century. *(Courtesy of Bryan Woodriff)*

Firth Park, April 2002. The triangular pond was drained during the Second World War. Its shape was retained and a concrete paddling pool was created. I can remember the paddling pool being used well into the 1960s. When travelling to Sheffield from Elsecar on the Upton to Sheffield bus, we passed through Firth Park. To me, then a small child, the paddling pool always looked so appealing, with children splashing around and sailing their boats. In more recent years Firth Park's attractiveness has waned. The gardens are a shadow of their former glory, the once popular paddling pool is now in a state of disrepair and has been drained to be used for basketball practice. Sadly neglected, Firth Park is typical of many municipal parks which have suffered greatly because of a lack of funding since local government changes in 1974. *(Paul T. Langley Welch)*

The clocktower,
refreshment rooms
nd gardens, Firth Park.
*(Courtesy of Bryan
Woodriff)*

The clocktower and refreshment rooms, Firth Park, April 2002.
(*Paul T. Langley Welch*)

Bellhouse Road, Firth Park, *c. 1912. (Courtesy of Bryan Woodriff)*

Bellhouse Road, Firth Park, mid-1950s. *(Courtesy of Bryan Woodriff)*

Bellhouse Road, Firth Park, April 2002. *(Paul T. Langley Welch)*

Concord Park, Shire Green, 1930s. The gates were the gift of Charles Boot, of Henry Boot & Sons Ltd, in 1932; they had originally stood at Hayes Park Place, Kent. Hayes Park Place was once the home of the distinguished statesman and our second prime minister, William Pitt, lst Earl of Chatham. *(Courtesy of Bryan Woodriff)*

Concord Park, April 2002. The cottage in Jacob's Lane (seen behind the gate in the picture above) and the farmhouse were demolished before the Second World War. The impressive gates still mark the entrance. I was delighted to visit Concord Park with Paul T. Langley Welch in order to photograph the gates as Paul's wife, Amanda, is the great-great-great-great-great-granddaughter of William Pitt, lst Earl of Chatham. *(Paul T. Langley Welch)*

Sycamore House Road, Shire Green, from Mason Lathe Road, 1930s. Until 1930 the land on which this council housing estate was built was farmland, the farmhouse being called Sycamore House Farm; it stood in the vicinity of the road junction seen here. It was last occupied by the Helliwell family. By 1933 the farmland had been filled by new roads and council houses. *(Courtesy of Bryan Woodriff)*

Sycamore House Road, Shire Green, from the same spot, April 2002. *(Paul T. Langley Welch)*

Shire Green Lane from the corner of Wincobank Avenue, late 1950s. The tall chimney belongs to the brickyard. *(Courtesy of Bryan Woodriff)*

The corner of Wincobank Lane in April 2002, showing the changes which have taken place in Shire Green Lane. The house in the right foreground is no longer a shop. The brickyard has gone and the modern building seen on the centre skyline is Ffolliott Bird Associates' dental practice. *(Paul T. Langley Welch)*

Shire Green Lane at its junction with Wincobank Road, 1960s. *(Courtesy of Bryan Woodriff)*

The junction of Shire Green Lane and Wincobank Road, April 2002. *(Paul T. Langley Welch)*

The junction of Fife Street and Ecclesfield Road from Barrow Road, Wincobank, March 1913. A single-decker Daimler omnibus can be seen approaching the Foundry Arms. *(Courtesy of Bryan Woodriff)*

The junction of Barrow Road, Wincobank, with Fife Street, April 2002. *(Paul T. Langley Welch)*

Kimberworth Hill can be seen rising above the Midland Railway bridge which passes over Fife Street, Wincobank, 17 March 1913. The Daimler omnibus is seen on the first day it went into service on the new bus route to Low Wincobank. *(Courtesy of Bryan Woodriff)*

Fife Street, Wincobank, April 2002. Blackburn and Wincobank Conservative Club can be seen on the right with its John Smith's Magnet Ales sign. The former business premises of Dewhurst's tailors and outfitters is in a semi-derelict state, further down the hill on the left. *(Paul T. Langley Welch)*

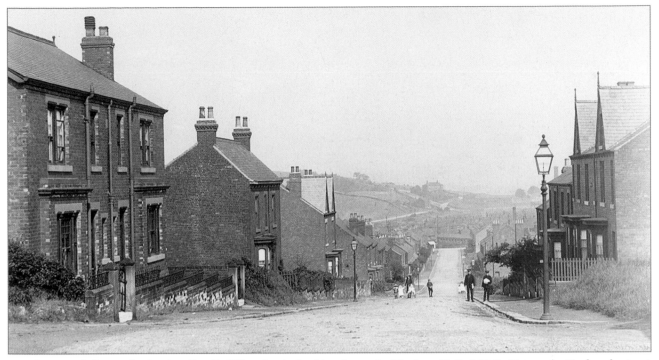

Standon Road (formerly Station Road), Wincobank, looking towards Meadow Hall, 1910. Stringer's Steelworks is at the bottom of the road. *(Courtesy of Bryan Woodriff)*

Standon Road, Wincobank, from the same spot, April 2002. Many of the Victorian houses seen on the left in the photograph above have been replaced by semi-detached 1930s houses. On the site of Stringer's Steelworks there is a gasworks; the large dome of a gas holder can be seen in its semi-deflated position. *(Paul T. Langley Welch)*

Attercliffe Common, 1970. The car outside the premises formerly occupied by the Blue Heaven Casino is a Sunbeam Rapier. *(Sheffield Central Library)*

Attercliffe Common, April 2002. The parade of shops seen above, along with many other shops, factories and houses, is now the site of Sheffield's prestigious Don Valley Stadium. *(Paul T. Langley Welch)*

Attercliffe Road, *c.* 1905. *(Sheffield Central Library)*

Attercliffe Road, April 2002. Part of the buildings seen on the left above, including no. 545, have been demolished. Highfield Motors occupies two former shops, including the premises of Entwistle & Son. The parade of shops between Entwistle's former premises and the Carlton public house has been replaced by modern buildings. The Dog and Partridge can be seen at the extreme end of the next parade of shops. *(Paul T. Langley Welch)*

A view down the Wallet End, Ecclesfield, *c.* 1906. Bank House, the home of the Greaves family, can be seen at the end of the street. *(Courtesy of Bryan Woodriff)*

The Wallet End, Ecclesfield, April 2002. Bank House, one of Ecclesfield's largest houses, is now the Regency Restaurant. *(Paul T. Langley Welch)*

A view of the Greyhound and Ball Inn, Ecclesfield, from the Wallet End, *c.* 1963. *(Courtesy of Cyril Slinn)*

The Greyhound and Ball Inn from the Wallet End shortly before sunset, April 2002. The building on the right forms part of the extension to Bank House, the Regency Restaurant. *(Paul T. Langley Welch)*

Priory Road, Ecclesfield. These eighteenth-century cottages and workshops stood at the bottom of Priory Road at its junction with Church Street. They were photographed by Cyril Slinn shortly before their demolition in 1972. *(Courtesy of Cyril Slinn)*

The site of the demolished eighteenth-century cottages and workshops in Priory Road, Ecclesfield, at its junction with Church Street, April 2002. *(Paul T. Langley Welch)*

The Village Reading Room and adjacent cottages, Church Street, Ecclesfield. The Village Reading Room was erected in 1722 on the site of an earlier wooden building which had been used as a school (records show repairs to this school in 1573). The building seen here served as a school until 1852 when it became a Mechanics' Institute. It was used by various village organisations until its demolition in 1972, shortly after Cyril Slinn took this photograph. *(Courtesy of Cyril Slinn)*

The site of the Village Reading Room and cottages in Church Street, Ecclesfield, April 2002. *(Paul T. Langley Welch)*

Ecclesfield Priory, late nineteenth century. After the Dissolution of the Monasteries by Henry VIII in 1539, Ecclesfield Priory and its 600 acres of land were given to Francis, 5th Earl of Shrewsbury, the lord of the manor. *(Courtesy of Bryan Woodriff)*

Ecclesfield Priory from St Mary's churchyard, April 2002. *(Paul T. Langley Welch)*

Stocks Hill, Ecclesfield, from Town End Road, 1906. The elegant gabled building with quoins, which dominates the centre back of the photograph, is the Feoffees Hall. A feoffee was a member of a board of trustees who administered land for charitable and public purposes. The history of the feoffees in Ecclesfield, of which there were originally fourteen, dates back to 1549. The hall seen here was built in the 1730s, and was demolished in 1968. A group of children pose for the photographer in front of the White Bear. In the group are Horace Hartley, with the basket, Florence Hemingfield and Mary Loxley, with the rolled-up pinafore in which she was carrying a cabbage, purchased on her way home from school. The old White Bear Inn was soon to be replaced by a new public house. *(Courtesy of Cyril Slinn)*

The 'new' White Bear Inn being constructed during the early years of the twentieth century. The 'old' White Bear Inn can be seen directly behind the new pub, to the left. *(Courtesy of Cyril Slinn)*

Stocks Hill from Town End Road, April 2002. *(Paul T. Langley Welch)*

Hill Top, Yew Lane, Ecclesfield, 1906. Occupants of the cottages on the right pose for the photographer. Left to right: Mrs Hartley, carrying Annie, and Mrs Susannah Witham, carrying Connie. In the right background Mrs Stringer stands in the road and Mrs Janet Johnson stands on the pavement next to her. In the doorway is Mr Colin Witham, while standing next to him is Jack Witham, aged three. He is crying because he wanted to go to the lavatory but had to wait until the photographer had finished. In the right foreground are Albert Beard and Ethel Green. The dog, Bellman, belonged to the Greens. *(Courtesy of Cyril Slinn)*

Hill Top, Yew Lane, April 2002, showing the location of the cottages seen in the above image. *(Paul T. Langley Welch)*

Hill Top, Yew Lane, Ecclesfield, 1972. Some of the cottages seen in the 1906 image opposite have already disappeared. This photograph was taken by Cyril Slinn shortly before the remaining cottages were demolished. *(Courtesy of Cyril Slinn)*

Hill Top, Yew Lane, April 2002, from the same spot as the photograph above. *(Paul T. Langley Welch)*

Hill Top, Yew Lane, Ecclesfield, 1964, from its junction with Stocks Hill and facing the opposite direction to the photographs on pages 90 and 91. *(Courtesy of Cyril Slinn)*

Hill Top, Yew Lane, Ecclesfield, from its junction with Stocks Hill, April 2002. *(Paul T. Langley Welch)*

The Black Bull, Church Street, Ecclesfield, *c.* 1908, believed to have been built in the sixteenth or early seventeenth century. The house on the right was built in 1770. Today the entire site is occupied by the new public house, also called the Black Bull. *(Courtesy of Cyril Slinn)*

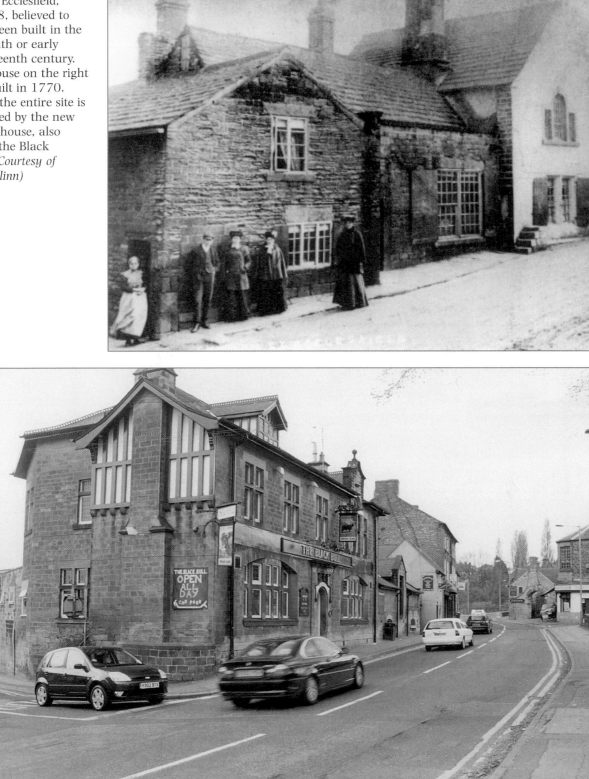

The Black Bull, Ecclesfield, April 2002. St Mary's Lane is on the left. *(Paul T. Langley Welch)*

A late-Victorian view showing old metalworkers' cottages and workshops in St Mary's Lane, Ecclesfield. This is a continuation of the Wallet (pages 84–5), leading to St Mary's parish church. *(Courtesy of Cyril Slinn)*

A similar view of St Mary's Lane, Ecclesfield, 1906. *(Courtesy of Bryan Woodriff)*

St Mary's Lane, Ecclesfield, towards the end of the Edwardian era. *(Courtesy of Cyril Slinn)*

St Mary's Lane, Ecclesfield, April 2002, Some striking changes have taken place in the intervening years since the previous three pictures were taken. *(Paul T. Langley Welch)*

Revd Dr Gatty (1813–1903) and his curate Mr Girling pictured on a lantern slide. Dr Gatty was the author of several books; his *Life At One Living*, published in 1884, records life in the village of Ecclesfield during his incumbency. His wife Margaret and his second daughter, Juliana Ewing, were very popular writers of children's stories. The Gattys had ten children. Margaret Gatty also wrote about seaweeds, zoophytes and sundials. She allowed herself to be chloroformed as an example for the parish. Juliana Ewing (1841–85) was a prolific writer and her children's stories were read all over the world. She had over two hundred stories, part-stories and poems as well as articles published in *Aunt Judy's Magazine*. Many were republished as separate story-books. In all she had thirty-three books published. In one story her invention of the Brownies inspired Baden-Powell to create a junior branch of the Girl Guides. Several of her stories were set in Ecclesfield, or elsewhere locally. *(Courtesy of Cyril Slinn)*

The interment of the Revd Dr Gatty in St Mary's churchyard. The celebrated Dr Gatty died on 20 January 1903 at the age of eighty-nine. He was Vicar of Ecclesfield from 1839 until his death, a total of sixty-three years. He married Margaret Scott (1809–73), daughter of Alexander John Scott, Chaplain to Lord Nelson at the Battle of Trafalgar, who cradled the dying admiral in his arms. Dr Gatty shares the same burial vault as his father-in-law. It is still a much-visited spot. *(Courtesy of Cyril Slinn)*

The Scott and Gatty tomb, April 2002. *(Paul T. Langley Welch)*

Church Street, Ecclesfield, in the early years of the twentieth century. The road has not yet been metalled. *(Courtesy of Bryan Woodriff)*

Church Street, Ecclesfield, *c.* 1912, looking northwards towards Mill Road. Note the recently metalled road. The early omnibus, known as Kitchener (named after the great British field marshal Lord Kitchener, 1850–1916), makes its way from Chapeltown to Firth Park via Ecclesfield village. *(Courtesy of Cyril Slinn)*

Church Street, Ecclesfield, April 2002. *(Paul T. Langley Welch)*

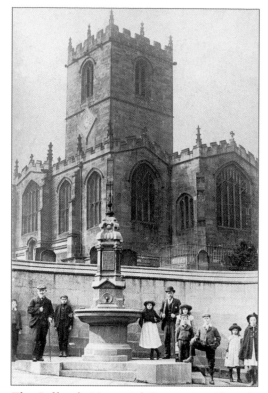

The Jeffcock Memorial Fountain, Church Street, Ecclesfield, was erected as a memorial to Thomas Jeffcock JP, DL, who died in August 1900 aged sixty. He was a local benefactor. In the photograph are Mr Wass, with walking stick, Mr Dunstal, wearing a bowler hat, and Florence Stringer. *(Courtesy of Cyril Slinn)*

Site of the Jeffcock Memorial Fountain, April 2002. Like many such fountains and water troughs throughout the area it has been removed, leaving a large recess in the churchyard wall which serves no useful purpose. *(Paul T. Langley Welch)*

The grave of Thomas Jeffcock in St Mary's churchyard, Ecclesfield, April 2002. *(Paul T. Langley Welch)*

Ecclesfield cinema from the end of Church Street, *c. 1925*. Built in 1920, it seated 685 patrons in stalls and balcony. Built and owned by Michael J. Gleeson, it opened on l June 1921 with the film *Broken Blossoms*, starring Lilian Gish. It closed during 1930, then reopened with sound on 7 March 1932, with *King of Jazz*. It was purchased by Essoldo on 11 September 1950 and closed its doors on 7 February 1959. The last film to be shown was *The Young Lions*, starring Marlon Brando. The Arundel Arms can be seen to the right of the cinema building. *(Courtesy of Cyril Slinn)*

A view from the end of Church Street, across The Common to the Arundel Arms, on whose car park once stood Ecclesfield cinema. The Arundel Arms is named after the Sussex home of the dukes of Norfolk, who have owned land in the area for centuries. *(Paul T. Langley Welch)*

Cote Lane, Ecclesfield, *c.* 1922. Ecclesfield cinema can be seen on the right. *(Courtesy of Cyril Slinn)*

The Common, formerly Cote Lane, Ecclesfield, April 2002. *(Paul T. Langley Welch)*

A late Victorian view of the Norfolk Arms, Penistone Road, Grenoside. *(Courtesy of Chris Sharp of Old Barnsley)*

The Norfolk Arms, Grenoside, April 2002. *(Paul T. Langley Welch)*

An early twentieth-century view of the Waggon and Horses, Burncross Road, Chapeltown. *(Courtesy of John R. Wrigley and Sheffield Central Library)*

A view of the former Waggon and Horses, Chapeltown, April 2002. Renamed Scandals, the former Waggon and Horses has recently undergone a facelift. To the right of the public house a parade of shops stands where the late Georgian buildings stood in the previous photograph. Above these shops is an Asda superstore. *(Paul T. Langley Welch)*

# 5
# The Eastern Outskirts

The George and Dragon, Beighton, *c.* 1900. Left to right: Mr Fitzaberley, Len Thompson senior, Mr Bartholomew, Frank Glover, who was killed in the First World War, and Mr Williamson.
*(Courtesy of Frank Money and Sheffield Central Library)*

Rotherham Road, Catcliffe, beyond which is the end of Whitehill Lane, *c.* 1905. On the right are the railings of Catcliffe Junior and Infant School. *(Courtesy of Chris Sharp of Old Barnsley)*

Situated east of the city of Sheffield about 4 miles from Rotherham, in a semi-rural location, Catcliffe had by the late nineteenth century fewer than one hundred houses in the village and until 1875 no public transport. St Mary's church was built in 1910. The adjacent tin mission church of St Faith was destroyed in the gales of 1962. One of Catcliffe's most striking features is one of the few remaining glass blowing kilns. South Yorkshire has a long tradition of glass making. The first was established in 1632 at Wentworth on land leased from Thomas Wentworth, lst Earl of Strafford (1593–1641). That particular enterprise did not survive long, but from the middle of the seventeenth century there were glassworks at Silkstone, near Barnsley, and Bolsterstone. William Fenny, who managed the glassworks at Bolsterstone in the early eighteenth century, fell out with his mother-in-law, the widow of its owner, who barred him in her will from making glass within 10 miles of Bolsterstone. He moved east to Catcliffe and in 1740 founded a new works making bottles, flint and window glass. He built two cone furnaces, one of which survives. The Catcliffe works was taken over by the May family in 1759 and from 1833 was run by Blunn & Booth. The works closed in 1884. Opening again very

The changed scene in 2002. The A630 crosses the Rotherham Road at Catcliffe. *(Paul T. Langley Welch)*

briefly in 1901, the works soon fell into a ruinous condition. The surviving cone was threatened with demolition in the 1960s. Restored, it is now a protected monument and is one of only five in the British Isles.

The first train to pass through Catcliffe was on the south-east line, Derby to Rotherham, in 1840. To the north the LNER station was built in 1875. As well as glassmaking, Catcliffe once had a diverse range of industries in which its inhabitants earned their livings; farming, strawberry growing and coal mining were the main occupations for local people. From 1875, with Catcliffe having its own railway station, new employment prospects opened up further afield. Today there is not a great deal of industry in Catcliffe itself, although the signs of its industrial past remain. This is the B6066 Rotherham Road, Catcliffe, April 2002. The cottages which were formerly on the left have been demolished. The land on which they stood is covered by the bridge which crosses the road, the A630, Sheffield Parkway, seen above. Just out of sight, the M1 motorway also crosses over the B6066 in Whitehill Lane.

Rotherham Road, Catcliffe, facing in the opposite direction to the previous two views, *c.* 1905. Just out of sight on the right-hand side is the Catcliffe glass cone. The Red Lion can be seen just before the railway bridge on the right. The tall gable of The Plough can be seen on the other side of the bridge. *(Courtesy of Chris Sharp of Old Barnsley)*

The B6066 Rotherham Road, Catcliffe, from the same spot, April 2002. Many of the buildings seen above have been demolished. The Red Lion is still intact, as is The Plough. *(Paul T. Langley Welch)*

The Market Cross, Woodhouse, *c.* 1900. *(Courtesy of Chris Sharp of Old Barnsley)*

The Market Cross, Woodhouse, April 2002. *(Paul T. Langley Welch)*

Station Road, Woodhouse, *c.* 1910: a very busy scene as the children go home from school. *(Courtesy of Chris Sharp of Old Barnsley)*

Station Road, Woodhouse, April 2002. *(Paul T. Langley Welch)*

# 6

# *Churches around Sheffield*

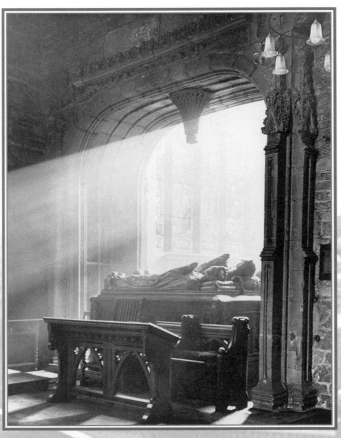

The cathedral church of St Peter and St Paul, Sheffield.
The Shrewsbury chapel, *c.* 1920. *(Sheffield Central Library)*

The parish church of St Peter, Sheffield, *c. 1910.* Most of the old cruciform church dates from the fifteenth century, although there are older fragments, including good stained glass, and part of a fourteenth-century Jesse window. The church was restored in the eighteenth century and again in 1880. *(Sheffield Central Library)*

A Supertram stops outside the cathedral. Twentieth-century additions to the former parish church of St Peter can be seen to the left. In 1914 Sheffield parish church was raised to cathedral status. Shortly after the end of the First World War the old parish church was enlarged. Twentieth-century additions include St George's chapel, the regimental chapel of the York and Lancaster Regiment, which was consecrated in 1966. *(Paul T. Langley Welch)*

Wadsley parish church. Built in 1834 through the generosity of the Misses Harrison, it was partly destroyed by fire in 1884 and reopened the following year. *(Courtesy of Chris Sharp of Old Barnsley)*

Wadsley parish church, seen here in April 2002. *(Paul T. Langley Welch)*

St Mary's church, Handsworth, *c.* 1905. The chancel, north chapel and lower part of the tower are thirteenth century but most of the rest dates from the nineteenth century. The octagonal tower top was added in 1825, the north aisle in 1833 and the south aisle in 1904. *(Courtesy of Chris Sharp of Old Barnsley)*

St Mary's church, Handsworth, April 2002. The church is currently undergoing an extensive restoration programme, supported by the National Lottery and the Heritage Lottery Fund. *(Paul T. Langley Welch)*

St Thomas's church, Wincobank, *c.* 1910. The church was built in Newman Road in 1875. Its appearance belies its age, possibly because of the clever use of materials, combined with 125 years or so of industrial grime. It is unlike many churches constructed during the nineteenth century, which were erected to a pattern specified by two Acts of Parliament, passed late in the reign of George III. These Acts of Parliament cited the Early English style of architecture as the preferred model. Unfortunately because of the rapidly expanding population due to increased industrialisation, it gave the South Yorkshire landscape more than its fair share of, although not boring, often fairly standard nineteenth-century church buildings. St Thomas's church, Wincobank, gives the impression that it has been standing for centuries, and makes a welcome change. *(Courtesy of Chris Sharp of Old Barnsley)*

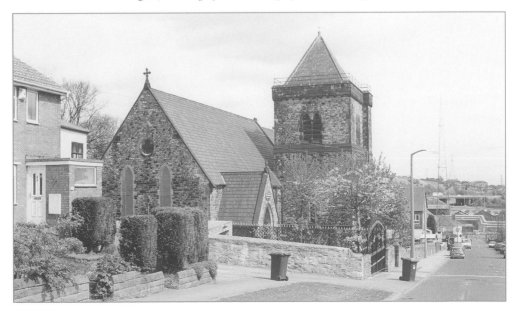

St Thomas's church,
Wincobank, April 2002.
*(Paul T. Langley Welch)*

This image is one of the earliest photographic images known to exist of Ecclesfield, or indeed anywhere. It is a collotype, the earliest form of photography, which preceded the daguerreotype. This image may date from as early as 1840, but certainly from before 1842, as it shows the parish church of St Mary, Ecclesfield, before the enlargement of the churchyard and the building of the bier house in 1842. The original was found being used as stiffening behind another picture. *(Courtesy of Cyril Slinn)*

St Mary's church, Ecclesfield, viewed from the same field as the collotype image, April 2002. More famously known as 'the Minster of the Moors', St Mary's parish once covered 78 square miles. Although parts of the building are earlier, the church is largely Perpendicular. There is some fifteenth- and sixteenth-century woodwork, including misericord stalls, screens and carved benches, as well as fragments of medieval stained glass. The colours, swords and bugles of the Ecclesfield Volunteers, raised to defend the area from attack by Napoleon, hang on the wall. *(Paul T. Langley Welch)*

The nineteenth-century parish church of The Ascension, Oughtibridge, *c.* 1910. *(Courtesy of Chris Sharp of Old Barnsley)*

The parish church of
The Ascension,
Oughtibridge, April 2002.
*Paul T. Langley Welch)*

Situated above Stocksbridge, the village of Bolsterstone stands 984 ft above sea level and is surrounded by spectacular scenery. Bolsterstone has had a succession of churches since the twelfth century. The present St Mary's was built in 1879. A list of incumbents is displayed in the church dating from 1412 to the present day. *(Courtesy of Chris Sharp of Old Barnsley)*

St Mary's church, Bolsterstone, April 2002. The village square is flanked by stone houses, the church, school and the Castle Inn. This inn was once owned by the celebrated performer Sam Costa, well known for his radio broadcasts, including *ITMA*. The inn is named after the castle built nearby by the Sheffield family in 1250, of which a few fragments remain. *(Paul T. Langley Welch)*

St Nicholas's church, Bradfield, *c.* 1905. This church was erected in 1109 by the Lovetot family, who had become lords of the manor during the reign of William the Conqueror. The Lovetots also built St Mary's church, Ecclesfield, to whose enormous parish this church became a chapel of ease until 1868. A square bell tower was added to the Norman structure in the fourteenth century before the church was enlarged and remodelled in the Gothic Perpendicular style of the fourteenth century. To the north of the main gates stands a watch house, built in 1831, to safeguard newly buried bodies from being anatomised. *(Courtesy of Chris Sharp of Old Barnsley)*

St Nicholas's church, Bradfield, April 2002. This church, which must surely be situated in one of the most picturesque locations in England, has sheep roaming freely in its gated churchyard. Its peal of eight bells was made by Taylors of Loughborough, six in 1847 and two in 1996. *(Paul T. Langley Welch)*

St Thomas Becket's church, Beauchief. This image shows part of the west end of Beauchief Abbey, founded in about 1175, and incorporated into the present-day church. Once situated in isolated splendour, Beauchief Abbey has been hemmed in by the sprawl of Sheffield's suburbs. Fortunately a golf course preserves some of the open landscape, but only a short lane leads from albeit attractive housing to this historic semi-ruin. (Bryan Woodriff Collection)

An interesting postcard view of the ruins of Beauchief Abbey. It is postmarked 7p.m., 5 June 1910. *(Bryan Woodriff Collection)*

An Edwardian postcard view of the tower of the church of St Thomas Becket, Beauchief, which forms the principal part of the once substantial Beauchief Abbey. *(Bryan Woodriff Collection)*

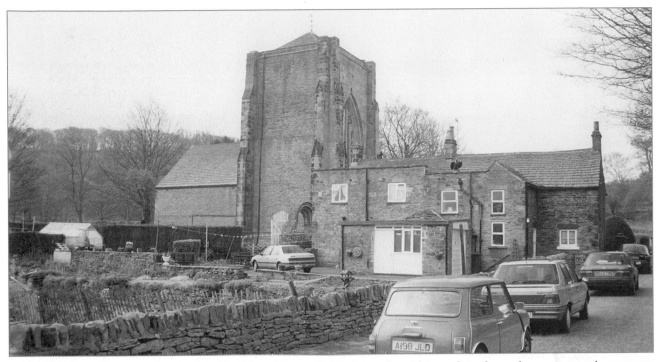

St Thomas Becket's church, Beauchief Abbey. Many of the better furnishings date from the seventeenth century. *(Paul T. Langley Welch)*

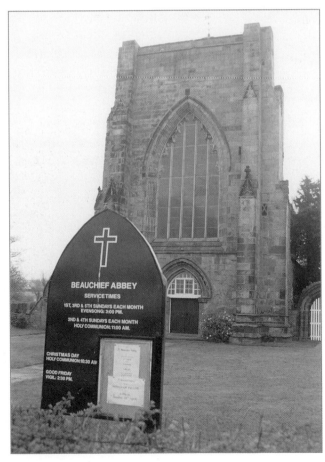

A close-up view of the west end of Beauchief Abbey, which incorporates the church of St Thomas Becket, seen here April 2002. *(Paul T. Langley Welch)*

# ACKNOWLEDGEMENTS

I am most grateful to: my personal assistant John D. Murray, John Bishop, Tony Briggs of Harvey & Richardson, Hoyland, Miss Tracy P. Deller, Ricki S. Deller, Miss Joanna C. Murray Deller, Brian Elliott, Mrs June Mary Firth, Doug Hindmarch, senior Local Studies Librarian at Sheffield Central Library, Mrs Joan Hopson, Mr Herbert and Mrs Doreen Howse, Frank Money, David J. Richardson, Chris Sharp of Old Barnsley (a shop specialising in local history in Barnsley's indoor market), Cyril Slinn, Mr David and Mrs Christine Walker of Walker's Newsagents, Hoyland, Mr Clifford and Mrs Margaret Willoughby, Bryan Woodriff, John R. Wrigley, and, at Sutton Publishing, Simon Fletcher and Michelle Tilling.

Paul T. Langley Welch, who took the present-day photographs of Sheffield included in this book, is a freelance commercial and theatrical photographer. Since 1983 he has worked for such companies as the National Theatre, the Old Vic, and the Royal Shakespeare Company. Commercial clients include United Distillers, the National Tourist Board, the Arts Council of Great Britain, British Telecom, and F1 Racing (Silverstone). He has also produced films in conjunction with Pauline Turner for PPM Productions, for the National Tourist Board. He has been honoured to photograph HRH Prince Philip, Duke of Edinburgh, the late HRH Princess Margaret, the Rt Hon. Tony Blair MP and the Rt Hon. William Hague MP, as well as hundreds of actors and actresses, including Dame Judi Dench, Dame Elizabeth Taylor, Sir Alec Guinness, and Alan Bates. He has been involved in projects with Geoffrey Howse since the 1980s and has photographed subjects for seven of Geoffrey's books. He and his wife Amanda have one daughter, Finn.